What's in a Name:
Fort Davis, Texas

Larry Francell

Purple Feather Press · Texas

Copyright © 2022 by Lawrence J. Francell All rights reserved.

Cover Illustration: Fort Davis, Harper's Weekly, March 1861. (Author's collection)

This book or any portion thereof may not be reproduced or used in any manner whatsoever without the express written permission of the publisher except for the use of brief quotations in a book review.

Printed in the United States of America

First Printing, October 2022

ISBN 978-1-7353805-3-7

Purple Feather Press
Texas

www.PurpleFeatherPress.com

What's in a Name:
Fort Davis, Texas

What's in a Name

Fort Davis, founded in 1854, was named after then Secretary of War Jefferson Davis. As we know, Davis went on to be the President of the Confederate States of America and directed the South during the War of the Rebellion. When the War ended and troops finally returned to the post on Limpia Creek, they continued the name Fort Davis, still the namesake of Jefferson Davis. At this time Davis was held as a military prisoner at Fortress Monroe off the coast of Florida and the troops who re-activated Fort Davis were the Buffalo Soldiers of the 9th Regiment of United States Cavalry. Why was the name never changed?

Larry Francell

Buffalo soldiers on Parade at Fort Davis. (Courtesy Fort Davis national Historic Site)

Not only were the returning troops African American, but their commanding officer, Lieutenant Colonel Wesley Merritt, was also an ardent Unionist. A generally quiet and reserved officer, Merritt was from New York and graduated West Point in 1860, joining the Second Dragoons, the US Army's version of Europe's heavy cavalry.

What's in a Name

Still in his 20s, Merritt was one of the more successful "boy generals" of the War, leading with distinction and gallantry at Brandy Station, the largest mounted battle ever waged in North America.

When the Rebels were finally chased out of their works before Petersburg, Merritt's cavalry was one of the units that pursued Lee all the way to Appomattox Courthouse and the ultimate surrender. He ended the War as commander of General Phillip Sheridan's corps of cavalry with the rank of Major General of Volunteers.

At the end of the War he, like many officers who decided to stay in the Army, was reduced in rank to Lieutenant Colonel and given the position of Second in Command of the Ninth Cavalry; the commanding officer being Colonel Edward Hatch, who in turn served under Benjamin Henry Grierson on his famous raid around the defenses of Vicksburg, but that's another story.

Larry Francell

*Lieutenant Colonel Wesley Merritt, 9th Cavalry, re-established Fort Davis June 9, 1867, and commanded the post until 1869.
(Courtesy Fort Davis National Historic Site)*

What's in a Name

Merritt and his men re-activated Fort Davis on June 29, 1867. Merritt continued to serve with distinction and rose to the rank of Major General, was for a time the Commandant of West Point and led the first Philippine Expeditionary Force in 1898 during the Spanish-American War.

If anyone had the motivation and opportunity to change the name of Fort Davis, it was Merritt. But he did not do so.

Larry Francell

Fort names from the period in the West are often interesting, sometimes unusual, sometimes mundane, and sometimes even obscure. We mostly think that heroes and geographic locations make up the norm, but in truth there is often no rhyme nor reason. There were several Fort Lincoln's as befitting the man who saved the Union.

Prior to Fort D. A. Russell in Marfa, Texas there was a Fort D.A. Russell in Wyoming near Cheyenne. David Allen Russell was a graduate of West Point who distinguished himself during the Mexican War and later the Peninsular Campaign, Gettysburg and the Wilderness dying during the Valley Campaign at Winchester, Virginia. Fort Sam Houston was named for a Texas hero, who did once serve in the U.S.

military as a volunteer and did serve in Congress. Fort Concho (1867) was named for the river where the post was located. Fort Worth was named for Department Commander William Jenkins Worth who fought in the Mexican War and died of cholera in 1849, certainly deserving the honor.

West of Fort Davis there was Fort Quitman (1858), named for Congressman and Mexican War hero John Quitman. Quitman was famous for exploits during the Mexican War, being the first man into the Citadel in Mexico City, having lost a shoe in the process. He was also appointed the military governor of Mexico City during the American occupation. Considered a contender for the presidency, he died shortly after attending the inauguration of James Buchanan. Many Southerners, because of his politics, were convinced that he had been poisoned but probably died of an illness much like Legionnaire's Disease.

Fort Bliss (1854) at El Paso was named for Lieutenant Colonel William W.S. Bliss, President Zachary Taylor's son-in-law who died in 1853. On the other hand, Fort Lancaster, my favorite Army post in West Texas, was named for a much lesser personality Job Roberts Hamilton Lancaster who had the bad luck to be struck and killed by lightening in 1841 during the Second Seminole War. Captain Stephen Carpenter, First Infantry, was assigned to build the post, and with boots on the ground was able to name the post for his friend.

Fort Stockton (1859) has an unusual history. Several sources state that the post was named for Commodore Robert Stockton, one of the instigators and leaders of the Bear Flag Revolt in California during the Mexican War. At the time Stockton was probably one of the most famous Navy commanders but naming an Army post after a Navy officer would be unusual and Commodore Stockton did not die until 1866. Forts were mostly named for dead people. Fort Stockton was actually named for Lieutenant Edward D. Stockton, from the First Infantry who died in 1857, the post being founded by a unit of the First Infantry from Fort Lancaster.

What's in a Name

Lieutenant Colonel Washington Seawell, 8th Infantry. Fort Davis was established by six companies of the 8th Infantry on October 7, 1854, and named for Secretary of State Jefferson Davis. Seawell, West Point, 1825, served as commanding officer of the fort for most of the pre-War period. (Courtesy Fort Davis National Historic Site)

Larry Francell

Fort Davis was founded on October 7, 1854, shortly after Lieutenant Colonel Washington Seawell, along with headquarters and six companies of the Eighth Infantry, arrived along Limpia Creek to establish a post to protect the overland trail to California and the gold fields. At that time and place it was more than appropriate and practically pre-ordained that the post be named for the Secretary of War, Jefferson F. Davis.

What's in a Name

⚓

Jefferson Finis Davis was born in Kentucky on June 3, 1808 but considered Mississippi home. It was from that state that he was appointed to West Point in 1824. Upon graduation, twenty-third in a class of thirty-two, he was commissioned a Second Lieutenant in the First Infantry. In 1832 Davis found himself serving under Colonel Zachary Taylor. He promptly fell in love with Taylor's daughter Sarah Knox Taylor and the couple was married in June 1835. Knowing the life of a transient Army wife, Davis resigned from the Army and the newlyweds intended to move to Mississippi where Davis would join his older brother as a cotton planter. However, within three months of the wedding both Davis and Sarah contracted malaria, and at age nineteen Sarah died on September 15, 1835.

Brother Joseph gave Davis 900 acres of adjoining land and starting with one slave he developed Brierfield Plantation. By 1845 he owned seventy-four slaves and was active in Mississippi politics winning election as a Representative to Congress in 1845. That same year he married seventeen-year-old Varina Banks Howell. A strong advocate of Southern rights and totally in favor of a war with Mexico, Davis resigned his seat in Congress in 1846 and accepted the governor's appointment as Colonel of the First Mississippi Rifles and marched for Mexico.

    Davis and his regiment participated in the siege of Monterrey and at the Battle of Buena Vista his regiment stopped an enemy cavalry charge cold. However, Davis was wounded in the foot, which ended his active military career, but not before convincing him that he had considerable military skill. Upon his return to Mississippi, he was appointed to fill an unexpired term in the U.S. Senate in 1847 and then was elected to a full term in his own right. In the Senate he advocated annexing all of northeastern

What's in a Name

Mexico and even Cuba to, as he said, "increase the number of slave holding constituencies."

Davis resigned from the Senate in 1851 to run for governor of Mississippi, but he lost that election. However, he was not out of government service long. In 1853 he was tapped by President Franklin Pierce as Secretary of War, a position he held with great distinction, and should he have stopped government service at that point he would be considered a great American rather than a traitor to his country.

As Secretary of War, Davis accomplished three things, one internal to the department, one a unique experiment in transportation, and one the greatest scientific endeavor the nation had undertaken since Lewis and Clark and the Corps of Discovery ventured West.

Fort Davis was named for Jefferson F. Davis, Secretary of War, shown here in the Mexican War uniform of a Major General of Volunteers. (Author's Collection)

What's in a Name

When Congress authorized the creation of two new regiments of infantry and two new regiments of cavalry, Davis used this to reorganize and modernize the US Army. Exchanging obsolete, but cheap weapons, for modern arms was one step. Under his watch West Point became the best engineering school in the country and Army officers more professional in their tasks. Davis took special care in the creation of the new Second Cavalry, which was assigned to the defense of the frontier in Texas. In time, the Second came to be known as "Jeff Davis's Own."

Larry Francell

It's important to understand that one of Davis's primary motives in everything he did was to promote Southern interests first and foremost. To this end his second accomplishment was an experiment to improve transportation in the desert Southwest. When he convinced Congress of the potential value of camels in 1855, $30,000 was appropriated for a test. The next year seventy-four camels arrived at Camp Verde, Texas and for the next several years they were used extensively. With the secession of the southern states these experiments ended, and the camels dispersed. By the end of the War and the completion of the transcontinental railroad, the much more reliable and faster mode of transportation took priority.

The last and most important of Davis's actions as Secretary of War was the first great and comprehensive reconnaissance of the American West,

What's in a Name

what is known as the Pacific Railway Surveys, or officially as *Reports of Explorations and Surveys to Ascertain the Most Practicable and Economic Route for a Railroad from the Mississippi River to the Pacific Ocean,* a long title but fitting for the first scientific survey of the American West.

The motivation for the Surveys was purely sectional. It was understood that, financially, there were only the resources to build one transcontinental railroad and both the North and the South, as well as the Middle Border, desired that the terminus be in their region. It was thought that science could solve the problem. In March 1853 Congress appropriated $100,000 and authorized the Secretary of War to undertake the surveys using the Army Corps of Topographical Engineers, the elite of West Point graduates. In all, four transcontinental routes were assessed, two in the south, one across the middle of the country and one to the north. At the same time another expedition undertook the task of surveying the various mountain passes in California through which a railroad must pass.

The Pacific Railway Surveys included reports on topography, geology, flora and fauna and even anthropological studies of Native Americans. Profusely illustrated, thirteen volumes were published in 1855, the first systematic analysis of the Great West. Barring other circumstances this alone should have established Davis's reputation. However, the Pacific Railway Surveys did not solve the problem of determining the route of the transcontinental railroad. In essence the men of the Army Corps of Topographical Engineers found several practical routes and the issue would not be decided until the South seceded from the Union, thereby withdrawing from the debate.

As we know, Sectionalism was the critical political issue at mid-19th Century. Davis was caught up in the debate, which changed the course of his place in history forever.

What's in a Name

Make no mistake, and no matter how the Southern Revisionist historians have twisted the facts, Jefferson Davis stood for slavery. Before the War he stated that slavery "was established by decree of Almighty God." He also wrote when describing the new Confederate government that, "its foundations are laid, its cornerstone rests, upon the great truth that the Negro is not equal to the white man; that slavery, subordination to the superior race, is his natural and moral condition."

Of course, after the War, Davis went to great lengths to try to rehabilitate himself relying on that favorite Southern refrain that the War was not about slavery but rather "state's rights." In essence the right of states to own slaves.

So here it is, and the question still remains: why did Wesley Merritt and the War Department keep the name Fort Davis?

Larry Francell

After the War of the Rebellion, veterans from both the North and the South organized themselves into fraternal and support organizations based upon the shared experience of war. I am reminded of the quote from veteran and Justice of the Supreme Court Oliver Wendell Holmes: "through our great good fortune in our youth our hearts were touched with fire." The Northern veteran's organization was called The Grand Army of the Republic (GAR). Fort Davis, located more western than southern and staffed by officers who fought in the War, quickly organized a chapter of the GAR. The name linked to the fort must have been strong for they named their group the Jefferson Davis Chapter. But this GAR Chapter was named for Jefferson Columbus Davis, not Jefferson Finis Davis.

There were two Jefferson Davis'.

What's in a Name

Jefferson Columbus Davis was born in Indiana and went through life known as "Jef," always signing his name that way. The only thing he ever wrote about his youth was that he, "was a good rider and accustomed to the use of horses." He had a lust for adventure and when the war with Mexico broke out, he joined the local Clark County Guards and, in the words of the day, marched off to "see the elephant."[1]

Davis distinguished himself as an enlisted man in the Mexican War and determined to remain in the Army as a career. However, without a West Point education he would always be looked down upon by his fellow career officers. In August 1848 he received a direct appointment as a Second Lieutenant in the First Regiment of Artillery, a most unusual circumstance in the day when our standing Army numbered fewer than 10,000, and direct appointments were exceedingly rare.

---

[1] Nathaniel Cheairs Hughes and Gorgon D. Whitney, *Jefferson Davis in Blue: The Life of Sherman's Relentless Warrior*, Baton Rouge: Louisiana State University Press, 2002), pp. 1-3.

Postings for West Point graduates were based upon class rank: the highest were offered the engineers, next in rank the artillery, then the cavalry, and last the infantry. The First Artillery was a distinguished unit and fellow officers included Thomas Jackson, A.P. Hill, John B. Magruder, Abner Doubleday and Robert Anderson among others who would gain prominence during the coming war.

The mission of the artillery was mostly coastal defense but as a junior officer Davis found himself serving in Florida during the Third Seminole War. Felled by yellow fever, he would suffer from recurring fevers throughout his life.

Jefferson Columbus Davis, Major General of Volunteers, Commanding XIV Corps on Sherman's March to the Sea. (Author's Collection)

Larry Francell

By 1861 he found himself serving as Major Robert Anderson's trusted confidant at Fort Sumter in Charleston, South Carolina harbor. When the Texan Louis Wigfall arrived to negotiate the surrender of the fort, Major Anderson was not at hand and, as Officer of the Day, Davis met him at the gate: "Your flag is down," (the pole having been shot through) stated Wigfall, "you are on fire and you are not firing your guns. General Beauregard (the Rebel commander) desires to stop this." "No sir, our flag is not down. It is for you to stop this," was the defiant reply marking Davis's attitude for the balance of the War.[2]

Davis spent his career in the Western Theater, beginning at Wilson's Creek (Elkhorn Tavern). It was here, as a division commander, he proved he could maneuver a large body of men aggressively and demonstrated an exceptional ability to swear creatively. At one point in the midst of this battle, a handsome riderless horse appeared through the smoke

---

[2] Ibid., p. 43.

crossing into Federal lines. He was caught and after the fight presented to Davis by the men of his old regiment, the Twenty-Second Indiana. Davis named him Skedaddle and this horse would stay with him throughout the War.

Davis fought his division at Corinth, Stone's River, Chickamauga and captured the city of Rome, Georgia during Sherman's Atlanta Campaign. On August 9, 1864, on the recommendation of General Sherman, Davis was given command of XIV (14th) Corps, the "Jeffs," as they came to call themselves, in time to lead one of Sherman's columns on the March to the Sea. He continued with Sherman through the Carolinas Campaign to the end of the War. Sherman wrote of Davis, "he threw his whole soul into the contest, and wherever the fighting was hardest we found him at the front."[3]

After the War, like many, Davis chose to stay in the Army and in 1867 was assigned as the commander

---

[3] Patricia Faust (editor), *Historical Times Illustrated Encyclopedia of the Civil War*, (New York: Harper/Collins, 1986), p. 208.

of the Department of Alaska. With no civilian government in place, he functioned as the civil authority as well. Headquartered at the old Russian capital of Sitka he had two companies (250 men) to control a region as large as Texas and California.

As the only government representative, it fell to Davis to establish U.S. authority. For the most part he proved a capable and generally fair administrator. When one of the local tribe members wounded a sentry over a disagreement, rather than start a major conflict, Davis marched alone into the native village and walked the miscreant out by the ear.

From 1870 to 1873, while nominally the Colonel of the Twenty-Third Infantry, he was assigned to the recruiting service spending three years in the East shuttling between New York and his home in Indianapolis. But in April 1873, Brigadier General Edward Canby was murdered in Oregon by the Modoc Indians. This was a small tribe forced onto the Klamath Reservation where they were bullied by the larger Klamath's. Under the leadership of tribal chief

Captain Jack, they jumped the reservation and took shelter in the Lava Beds near Tule Lake in northern California. It was there during peace negotiations that Canby and another man were killed.

Davis was assigned field command to end the Modoc War, which he brought to a satisfactory conclusion from the Army's standpoint, at least. In declining health, he would spend the rest of his military career often on sick leave or inactive. He died on November 30, 1879.

It would seem from this record that Jefferson C. Davis might well have been an acceptable namesake for Fort Davis as the Federal troops returned. But this Davis had two black marks that could never be erased.

Other than in time of war, the first would have ended any career. On September 29, 1862, Davis murdered a superior officer in cold blood. General William "Bull" Nelson was in command of Louisville, Kentucky, which was threatened by Rebel siege. Davis was sent to assist in the defense of the city. Nelson was described by one soldier as the "best, finest and most elegant and original swearer in the whole United States Army – rivaling Jef C. Davis."[4]

Davis, always sensitive to his lack of West Point training and the fact that he was a regular Army officer and not a volunteer, as were most, took umbrage at a comment by Nelson. Nelson had assigned Davis to establish a "home guard" in the defense of Louisville. Based upon his rank and experience Davis did not take well to the task, describing the men he found as "squirrel hunters and people picked off the streets." By all accounts Davis did not exert himself in this exercise and was summoned by Nelson to his headquarters at the Galt House.

Incensed, Davis proceeded immediately to headquarters where he and Nelson entered into a lively exchange. At one point Davis stated, "General Nelson, I am a regular soldier, and I demand the treatment due me as a general officer." Thereupon

---

[4] Hughes & Whitney, p. 104.

What's in a Name

Nelson relieved Davis of duty turning to his adjutant Captain Miles Kendrick, "Captain, if General Davis does not leave the city by nine o'clock tonight, give instructions to the Provost-Marshal to see that he shall be put across the Ohio."

Davis left the city as ordered, but when Union general Don Carlos Buell relieved the siege of the city, Davis returned to reclaim command of his division. Buell proceeded to make matters worse when he assigned Davis's Ninth Division to the Third Corps commanded by Nelson.

On the morning of September 29, 1862, Bull Nelson was in the lobby of the Galt House after his breakfast. There he was confronted by Jef Davis, "I want you to know you have disgraced me." Nelson replied, "do you know who you are talking to sir." And then, "Go away you damned puppy. I don't want to have anything to do with you." Whereupon an infuriated Davis flipped a visiting card in Nelson's face. Nelson in turn slapped Davis. Davis demanded an apology, but Nelson slapped him again and called him a coward. "I will see you again," said Davis as he stormed off.

Davis then entered the dining room where he borrowed a "Tranter" revolver from his friend Colonel Tom Gibson. As Davis marched off, Gibson told him, "It's a tranter, work light." Davis confronted Nelson near the staircase. Both men were raging mad, but Nelson was unarmed. Davis fired once hitting Nelson just above the heart. Nelson struggled up the stairs to the first-floor landing and collapsed, asking, "send for a clergyman, I wish to be baptized, I have been basely murdered." Moved to an adjacent room Nelson was baptized by the Reverend Jeremiah Talbott of the Calvary Episcopal Church before he died.[5]

One might imagine that something of this magnitude would have major repercussions, but it did not for several reasons. Davis was well liked by the common soldiers. Nelson not so much. When the news reached the 105th Ohio, the men at parade cheered.

---

[5] All quoted material in the preceding paragraphs is from Hughes and Whitney, *Jefferson Davis in Blue*, pp. 112-116.

What's in a Name

"Why are those men cheering," one officer asked. "The men are cheering Gen. Jef C. Davis, sir," was the reply. An officer in another regiment recorded, "Gen. Nelson shot. Soldiers shed no tears for him."

Immediately after the incident Davis explained his actions. "I had to do it. I belong to the Regular Army and to not resent an insult of that kind would have been to make me shunned by all my brother officers. I must either call him to account or be as the dog that sleeps under my father's floor. I regret the necessity, but I could not have done otherwise."[6]

At the same time General Don Carlos Buell was in command of the department, and never expeditious in the handling of his army, was relieved of command and replaced by General George H. Thomas. In Thomas's mind, the Nelson death was Buell's problem, not his, and besides he needed men who knew how to fight. Davis was soon restored to duty.

The second black mark on his record occurred during Sherman's March to the Sea. As the army

---

[6] Ibid., p. 119.

marched towards Savannah, large numbers of newly freed slaves attached themselves to the moving columns of Federals, including Davis's. Never fully sympathetic to their plight, on December 9, 1864 at Ebenezer Creek, Davis ordered the pontoon bridge used for crossing to be removed before the refugees could cross. Several hundred were captured by Rebel forces and many drowned attempting to escape. As with the Nelson Affair the intensity of the conflict ensured there were no repercussions.

Upon his death, John Bourke, a fellow comrade in arms, wrote, "Jefferson C. Davis was one of the bravest and most efficient and energetic officers of the late war."[7]

A more personal and descriptive description of Davis was rendered by Will Z. Corin, one of the soldiers under Davis's command: "[Davis] has sandy hair and whiskers and an eye that can look through a stone wall. He has an awful wicked look but is the idol

---

[7] Ibid., p. 415.

What's in a Name

of the Corps – because he is brave and sharp ... feeds his corps better than any other corps commander can. He wore a slouched hat pulled down over one eye (he always does) so that he could just cock one eye on us."[8] However, he was a man ever tainted by the murder of Bull Nelson and Ebenezer Creek, and an officer who never rose above the permanent rank of colonel in the Regular Army. While it was fitting that the Fort Davis GAR take his name for their post, it is not surprising that, even had he been dead at this point, he would not ever be the man for which the fort would be named when the Army returned to Limpia Creek in 1867.

---

[8] Ibid., p. 318.

Larry Francell

But the story does not end here. There were efforts to change the name of Fort Davis. The strongest voice in this endeavor was that of General James Carleton. Like many officers after the War, Carleton reverted in rank to Lieutenant Colonel of the Fourth Regiment of Cavalry, but in 1871 he was Acting Inspector General of the Army.

An ardent Unionist, Carleton was one of the most colorful and respected officers in an Army that had plenty of characters. Born in Maine, he was commissioned out of the enlisted ranks during the Aroostook War of 1838. He went West with the 2nd Dragoons and like many others made his reputation in the Mexican War. By 1861, with experience as a frontiersman and Indian fighter, Carleton was promoted from captain to the colonel of the First

California Volunteers, and then to commander of the District of Southern California. It was in this capacity that he led the California Column east to counter the Confederate invasion of New Mexico. The Rebels, under General Henry Hopkins Sibley, were repulsed at the Battle of Apache Pass (Glorieta) before Carleton arrived, where upon he was placed in command of the Department of New Mexico.

With the Rebel threat gone, Carleton turned his attention to what was considered the "Indian problem," which had plagued New Mexico since the Spanish arrived. He was most famous, or probably infamous, for sending Kit Cason and troops to invade Canyon de Chelly and sending the Navajo on their "Long Walk" to Fort Sumner and the Bosque Redondo reservation where they languished until 1868.

Among his other interests Carleton aspired to be a writer and when younger even corresponded with Charles Dickens about his literary desires. He did publish several books including a history of the Mexican War. His inspection report on Fort Davis runs many pages and is the most thorough of the several I have read.

But it is his strong negative feelings about the name Fort Davis that come to the fore. Immediately he writes, "the name should be changed." Then, "I hope this matter will receive consideration and action."

Fort Davis towards the end of its existence as a U.S. Army post. The fort was de-activated in June 1891. (Courtesy Fort Davis National Historic Site)

What's in a Name

Carleton even has a solution, "I would suggest that it be called Fort B.F. Davis in honor of Col. Benjamin F. Davis, of the 8th New York Cavalry in the service of the United States. Col. Davis was a graduate of West Point and was appointed from Mississippi. He stood by the colors and fell in their defense. The other Davis [which he carefully underlines for emphasis], no relation of his, does not have the unsullied record of this young patriot."[9]

Carleton had enough experience, many friends at the highest level of the Army command, and enough force of personality that one would think that his recommendation to change the name would carry enough weight. But evidently not.

So, what can we conclude? Not much. There is no answer, as yet, as to why the name Fort Davis was not changed in 1867. I suspect it was a case of inertia and an Army bureaucracy very busy elsewhere. I

---

[9] Lt. Col. James Charleton, Acting Inspector General U. S. Army, *Report on Fort Davis, Texas, 1871*, (Archives File, Fort Davis National Historic Site).

doubt it had anything to do with reconciliation; Jefferson Davis, though soon released from custody at Fortress Monroe, was still considered a traitor in the North and Reconstruction was being applied full bore on the South by the Radical Republicans.

This is what we can appreciate about history and historical research; the answer may be out there somewhere so one just keeps looking. Like the fact that there happened to be two Jefferson Davis', there is always something interesting to discover even if it is not what one is initially seeking.

What's in a Name

Epilogue

There is a difference between the remembrance of history and the reverence of it.
- Mitch Landrieu, Mayor of New Orleans

There is a crack in everything. That's how the light gets in.
- Leonard Cohen

We are often asked by well-intending folk, and some not so well-intending, why do we not change the name. But what should we change, and how? The Davis Mountains? The town of Fort Davis? Jeff Davis County? Fort Davis National Historic Site? Or all?

The last is most problematic. The old fort was named for Jefferson Davis when he was Secretary of War, and the name carries on through history to a National Historic Site, "national" being the key word. While named for a traitor to his country, but not at the time of its establishment, the post-Civil War fort can well be considered the home of the Buffalo Soldiers, the African American soldiers who served on the frontier.

Larry Francell

The fort also serves to tell the story of the conflict between Native Americans, with a tide of settlers always pushing against the frontier, what the Apache's considered their homeland. We must think of those Buffalo Soldiers who were caught between the original inhabitants of the land and the constant pressure of the mostly white usurpers. Did the Buffalo Soldiers dwell on the name of the post where they served, or did they merely do their duty?

The contemporary conflict over statues and monuments centers around a period in American history known as the Jim Crow era, the early decades of the 20th Century at the height of the "Lost Cause" theory falsely promulgated by Southern historians and politicians. As Mitch Landrieu writes, "The statues were not honoring history, or heroes. They were created as political weapons, part of an effort to hide the truth, which is that the Confederacy was on the wrong side of humanity." These monuments were not about history but about control.

What's in a Name

Fort Davis was established in 1854, six years before the Civil War and decades before monuments and Jim Crow. Context is important and we cannot judge what our forefathers did in light of modern thought. This does history a disservice: we need to remember history not revere it.

My grandfather arrived from Lithuania at the height of Jim Crow. My grandmother arrived from Poland at the same time. They met in Chicago and made a life there. My father came to Texas during World War II as a member of the U.S. Army Air Corps where he met my mother at a USO dance in Odessa, Texas.

My mother's great uncle's family was on these shores for generations before he enlisted in the 39th Georgia Volunteers where he fought at Vicksburg, Missionary Ridge, and Franklin, surrendering at Durham Station after Appomattox. In the process he saved the regimental battle flag, which now resides in the museum in Dalton, Georgia. He fought for the wrong cause, but I am proud of both sides of my family and like many Americans, I have both deep roots and a recent immigrant past.

Fort Davis was named for a person, who at the time, was doing great things for his country. At this place where I live, the press of frontier settlement, the conflict between Black soldiers, many former slaves, (and their white officers) and the indigenous population of Native Americans, and a controversial and deeply flawed Jefferson Davis come together to tell a truly American story. A story that needs more light, not less.

As always, I thank Dr. Edward Hake Phillips of Austin College as my mentor, friend, and teacher.

Bibliography

Carleton, Lt. Col. James (Acting Inspector, U.S. Army). *Inspection Report, Fort Davis, Texas, January 1871.* Records File, Fort Davis National Historic Site.

Faust, Patricia (Editor). *Historical Times Encyclopedia of the Civil War.* New York: HarperCollins Publishers, 1991.

Frazer, Robert W. *Forts of the West.* Norman: University of Oklahoma Press, 1965.

Girardi, Robert L. *The Civil War Generals: Comrades, Peers, Rivals in Their Own Words.* Minneapolis: Zenith Press, 2013.

Goetzman, William. *Exploration and Empire: The Explorer and the Scientist in the Winning of the American West.* New York: Alfred A. Knopf, 1967.

Heitman, Francis. *Historical Register and Dictionary of the United States Army, 1789-1902.* (Vol. I) Urbana: University of Illinois Press, 1965.

Hughes, Nathaniel Chairs, Jr. and Gordon Whitney. *Jefferson Davis in Blue: The Life of Sherman's Relentless Warrior.* Baton Rouge: University of Louisiana Press, 2002.

Ovies, Adolfo. *The Boy Generals: George Custer, Wesley Merritt, and the Cavalry Of the Army of the Potomac.* El Dorado Hills, California: Savas Beatie Press, 2021.

Larry Francell

Utley, Robert M. *Special Report on Fort Davis, Texas.* Santa Fe: National Park Service, 1960.

What's in a Name

About the Author

Larry Francell has degrees in history from Austin College (B.A. – thank you Dr. Ed Phillips) and UT-Austin (M.A.) and began a 50-year career in museums as a summer ranger at Fort Davis National Historic Site.

For the past 20 years he has also been involved in Jeff Davis County government in several elected and appointed positions. He is the author of *Fort Lancaster: Texas Frontier Sentinel, Fort Davis (Images of America), How Indian Emily Saved Fort Davis* and the Introductory Essay of *Marfa Flights* by Paul Chaplo.

He has always been intrigued by why the Army never changed the name of Fort Davis, and even though he must have been a perplexing and challenging character, has a much greater affinity for Jefferson C. Davis than the other guy.

www.ingramcontent.com/pod-product-compliance
Lightning Source LLC
Chambersburg PA
CBHW071255070526
44583CB00017B/2481